HOW BOOKS ARE MADE

A TRUE BOOK

by

Lucia Raatma

Children's Press®
A Division of Grolier Publishing
New York London Hong Kong Sydney
Danbury, Connecticut

Reading Consultant
Linda Cornwell
Learning Resource Consultant
Indiana Department
of Education

An author doing research

Visit Children's Press on the Internet at:
http://publishing.grolier.com

Library of Congress Cataloging-in-Publication Data

Raatma, Lucia.
    How books are made / by Lucia Raatma.
        p.   cm. — (A True book)
    Includes bibliographical references and index.
    Summary: Describes the process of making a book including the work
done by authors, editors, proofreaders, designers, and printers.
    ISBN 0-516-20671-0
    1. Publishers and publishing—Juvenile literature. [1. Publishers and
publishing. 2. Books.] I. Title. II. Series.
Z278.R23   1998
070.5—dc21   97-26103
                                                                   CIP
                                                                   AC

Contents

It Starts with an Idea

Every book begins with an idea. An author has an idea to write about, or maybe an editor suggests an idea to an author. Either way, the idea is the beginning of a big process.

Once an author writes down his idea and turns it

into a manuscript, he submits it to an editor. The editor reads the manuscript to make sure it is the right length and to make sure everything is said in the best way. She makes any changes that are

An author sending his manuscript to a publishing house

The editor reads the manuscript and makes any necessary changes (left). The editor and author then discuss the manuscript (right).

necessary. This is called editing.
The editor and the author
discuss these changes.

The editor and author choosing illustrations for the book

If the book will include illustrations, the editor and the author talk about where to get them. Sometimes an author draws his own pictures. Other times, the editor hires

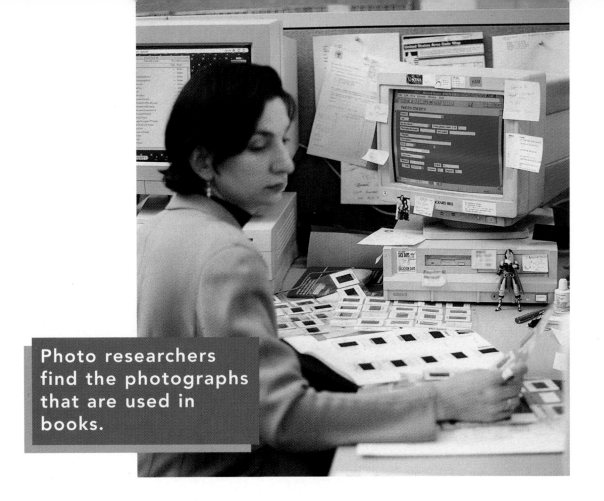

Photo researchers find the photographs that are used in books.

someone else to draw them. And in other instances, books are illustrated with photographs found by people who work in the editor's office.

The People in a Publishing House

An editor is but one of many people who work for a publisher. Publishing "houses," as they are called, are made up of editors, designers, and artists, as well as people who sell the books and plan for them. Certain people decide what time of year a book

The marketing team (left) figures out how to make people want to buy the book. The production team (right) keeps track of the schedule and quality of the book.

should be published. Others decide how much a book should cost. All of these people work very hard to make an author's idea into the best book possible.

Preparing the Words

After the editor and the author are happy with the manuscript, they give it to a copy editor. This person reads the manuscript to make sure all the grammar is correct and that every word is spelled correctly. At the same time, a fact checker reads the manuscript and

A copy editor checks the manuscript for correct grammar and spelling.

makes sure everything the author has written is true.

The final version of the manuscript is typed into a computer

The editor works on the final version of the manuscript on her computer.

and transferred to a computer disk. The editor then sends the computer disk to the designer. Meanwhile, the illustrations are prepared so that the designer can work with them.

Preparing the Pictures

Before the designer can work with the pictures, they must be sent to a color separator. The color separator places each picture on a machine called a scanner. The scanner electronically converts the pictures into images that can later be called up on the designer's computer.

The illustrations for the book are placed on a scanner.

Believe it or not, most color pictures are a combination of just four colors: cyan, magenta, yellow, and black. The scanner is able to divide an illustration into each of its

16

Color pictures are made up of four colors: cyan, magenta, yellow, and black.

four basic colors. It then creates
an electronic computer file of
the picture.

The computer file is sent to a
machine that creates four pieces
of film, each one representing

A photograph with only its yellow parts, and then with its magenta, cyan, and black parts added

one of the four colors. The four films are put together, and a color proof is made. Then the separator sends the color proofs and computer files of all the pictures to the designer.

Putting Words and Pictures Together

Once the designer has received both the scanned pictures and a computer disk of the manuscript, he can begin to design the book.

The designer decides where each illustration should go within the book and chooses what fonts to use for the words. He

On a computer, the designer plans how the book will look.

also decides how the book's cover should look.

Many years ago, the designer had to design the book by hand-pasting columns of text around the pictures. Today, designers can do this on computer, which means that making changes is a lot easier.

The designer puts the computer files of the manuscript and the illustrations into his computer. Now he can work with both the text and the pictures on his computer.

The editor and the designer look at a proof of the book's cover.

Fonts

A font is the kind of type used in a book. There are thousands of different fonts. Some are serious, some are playful, some are very elegant, some are fun. Fonts can give the book a certain feeling, so the designer chooses fonts carefully. If you have used a computer, you may have used different fonts.

The quick brown fox jumped over the lazy dog's back.

The quick brown
fox jumped over
the lazy dog's back.

*The quick brown fox jumped
over the lazy dog's back.*

The quick brown
fox jumped over the
lazy dog's back.

The quick brown fox jumped
over the lazy dog's back.

These are a few of the thousands of
fonts used by book designers.

Page Proofs

Once the text and the pictures are in place, the designer prints out page proofs from the computer. This is a set of pages that look just like book pages, but they are still loose.

A proofreader carefully reads the page proofs to make sure no words have been left

The editor checking page proofs (left) and page proofs with corrections marked on them (below)

Trim o.k.?

China's largest cities include Beijing, (the nation's capital), as well as Shanghai, Tianjin, and Guangzhou. Because the cities are so crowded, the government controls the number of people who may live there.

The city of Beijing is the capital of China.

Enlarge photo

Shanghai, Tianjin, and Guangzhou. Because the cities are so crowded, the government controls the number of people who may live there.

The city of Beijing is the capital of China.

out or spelled incorrectly. At this point, the author reads these proofs too. This is his last chance to make any changes to his text.

Once the editor, proofreader, and author are happy with the page proofs, they give them back to the designer. He makes sure all the pictures are in the right places, and that the text and pictures look nice together. Then any necessary changes are made on the computer.

The next stage is called second proofs. This set of proofs should include all the changes requested in the last stage. The editor makes sure all the changes were made correctly. She may even ask a proofreader to read the text again to be sure nothing was missed.

Once the pages are per-fect, a final version is copied from the designer's computer onto a computer disk. This disk and a copy of the pages are submitted, with all the illustrations, to the production department.

Along the way, the production department has done a cost estimate. An estimate includes all the items that the publisher will spend money on to produce the book. The production department then orders paper for the book.

At this point, the author's good idea—now close to

A person in the production department figures out the cost of making the book.

becoming a book—leaves the publishing house and goes back to the color separator.

On Press at the Printer

The production department sends the final computer disk back to the color separator. Using the disk, the color separator combines the text and pictures and then creates sheets of film that represent each complete page of the book.

At the color separator's office, the text and photos are merged on the computer.

The separator produces a set of pages from the film called bluelines. This is a full set of pages with all the pictures in place. They are called bluelines, or blues, because

Matchprints and bluelines

they are actually blue in color. The separator also produces full-color sheets called Matchprints.

The editor, designer, and production manager check the blues for any mistakes. They

check the Matchprints to make
sure all the colors are correct.
Then the film is sent to the
printer.

The editor makes
corrections on the
Matchprints (right).
The color separator
discusses corrections
made on the
Matchprints by the
editor (below).

The printer uses the film to make final printing plates in sections called signatures. These signatures are made of either sixteen or thirty-two pages all laid out on one big sheet that prints on both sides.

The plates are put on big cylinders of a printing press. Paper sheets called press sheets are printed out. Many copies of the press sheets are

Press sheets coming out of the printing press

A worker checks
a press sheet.

made. The individual big
sheets are then folded. They
are gathered with other signatures from the same book,
and the edges are trimmed.

This is how the pages look after they are bound, but before the cover has been glued on.

Then the printed pages are sent to the bindery. There the pages are bound together and glued to the case that holds the book in place. Sometimes

The editor checks the completed book.

the case has the cover illustration on it. Other times, the case is one color and a paper jacket is wrapped around it.

Once the case and the jacket are in place, you have a finished book!

Into the Bookstores and Libraries

As each book is being written and produced, the sales people from the publishing house have been telling everyone about it. They explain what the book is about and ask their accounts—the bookstores and libraries—to buy the book. The owner of a bookstore will decide how many copies she would like. A librarian decides if he will buy this book for his library.

Meanwhile, other people from the marketing department get attention for the book. They send out copies so magazines will review the book, and they create advertisements for newspapers. Sometimes, they even have the author come to a bookstore to sign copies for his readers.

Warehouse workers get books ready to be shipped to stores and libraries.

When a book is finished, all the copies are sent to a warehouse. From there, they are shipped to stores and to libraries. Once a book reaches the bookstore or library, it is

A librarian shelves a new book in its proper place.

put in the proper section. Picture books are kept in a place different from biographies. And books about sports are kept in a place different from cookbooks.

If you are looking for a book to read, just go to the section that interests you. There you'll find somebody's good idea just waiting for you to read it.

To Find Out More

Here are some additional resources to help you learn more about how books are made:

 **Books**

Aliki. **How a Book Is Made.** Crowell, 1986.

Kalman, Bobbie. **How a Book Is Published.** Crabtree, 1995.

Robins, Deri, and Charlotte Stowell. **Making Books.** Kingfisher, 1994.

Swain, Gwenyth. **Bookworks: Making Books by Hand.** Lerner, 1995.

Organizations and Online Sites

The Bookbinder's Guild of New York

c/o W.H. Freeman and Co.
41 Madison Avenue
New York, NY 10010

This organization provides information on traditional and modern bookbinding.

The Children's Book Council

568 Broadway, Suite 404
New York, NY 10012
http://www.cbcbooks.org

A group that provides a wealth of information about book publishing and children's books.

The Children's Book Guild

http://www.childrensbookguild .org
An organization of authors, artists, and editors involved in making children's books.

Children's Literature

http://www.childrenslit.com
A website with reviews and information about children's books.

The Internet Public Library

http://ipl.org/youth
Enter the IPL's Reading Zone link to find interviews with authors, children's writing and more.

Important Words

bindery place where the pages of a book are bound together and glued to the book's cover

color separator person who uses a scanner to change a four-color piece of art into four different versions, showing only one color in each version

cylinder rotating part of a printing press

font particular design of type; the font used for this book is called Avenir

manuscript handwritten or typed piece of writing that has not yet been published

merged combined

proofs early samples of pages produced during the making of a book; these are checked by the editor to make sure all mistakes are fixed before the final version of the book is printed

Index

Meet the Author

Lucia Raatma spent many years in book publishing before becoming a free-lance writer. She lives with her family in New York State.